ATLANTIC EDITIONS draw from *The Atlantic*'s rich literary history and robust coverage of the driving cultural and political forces of today. Each book features long-form journalism by *Atlantic* writers devoted to a single topic, focusing on contemporary articles or classic storytelling from the magazine's 165-year archive.

ON
MISDIRECTION

Magic, Mayhem, American Politics

MEGAN GARBER

zando
NEW YORK

Zando
zandoprojects.com

First Edition: January 2023

Text and cover design by Oliver Munday

The publisher does not have control over and is not responsible
for author or other third-party websites (or their content).

Library of Congress Control Number: 2022939754

978-1-63893-062-4 (Paperback)
978-1-63893-063-1 (ebook)

10   9   8   7   6   5   4   3   2   1
Manufactured in the United States of America

CONTENTS

Introduction   vii

Are We Having Too Much Fun?   1

The Great Fracturing of American Attention   13

How to Look Away   25

Boredom Is Winning   33

Do You Speak Fox?   45

Dwight Schrute Was a Warning   59

Beware False Endings   71

American Cynicism Has Reached a Breaking Point   77

Article Credits   91

About the Author   92

INTRODUCTION

———

I still remember the first time I connected to the internet. The modem screeched, the hulking computer practically shuddered with effort, and the pixelated images took approximately five lifetimes to load. It felt like magic.

For a while, the internet remained like that for me: It was a portal to the world, giddy and pulsing with possibility. It was connection to other people. It was knowledge. It was fun. The essays in this collection are, in one way, attempts to explore what happened in the internet's aftermath: how something with so much magic could bring with it so much menace. The essays are not directly about the web; most of them, instead, focus on other mediums (print news, TV news, books, the NBC sitcom *The Office*). But each is an attempt to make sense of the media environment that the internet—and, in particular, social media—have created: one in which people are empowered to broadcast themselves and their experiences in ways never before possible . . . but in which, too, they are often flattened and dehumanized, treated not as people at all, but as characters in ongoing melodramas.

The internet is a medium of exposure. Every day it compounds our awareness of each other, bringing new information and stories and opinions, all of it spinning and blurring and tangling. These essays consider what it feels like to live within that churn. They consider how people cope with the tumult. And they acknowledge how tempting it can be, in a world of ceaseless more-ness, to seek refuge in easy distractions. The essays' unifying theme is "misdirection," and the term's double meaning is, I think, illustrative: Misdirection suggests both the workings of magic—sleights of hand, cunning diversions—and paths gone awry. It suggests all the ways that people can be convinced to look through the things that are happening right in front of them. And it suggests, too, the dire consequences of all those averted eyes. "Misdirection," to me, is a reminder of all that can go wrong when people are able to look at the world without really seeing it.

These essays give shape to those failures of vision. They examine, in particular, how people in power have engaged in strategic sleights, distracting us and beguiling us and doing all they can to keep us from acknowledging what is plain. One essay, "Boredom Is Winning," written during Donald Trump's first impeachment, looks at the ways apathy was summoned, during that trial, as a political argument. Another, "How to Look Away," studies the tactics that politicians and pundits used as they told people not to care about the children who had been torn from their families at the southern border. Such grim illusions are becoming more and more common in America. They

A

treat people as spectacles, and judge human events solely according to their capacity to entertain. They warn of a society, as the collection's final essay argues, that risks collapsing under the weight of its own cynicism.

This collection covers a range of dates. The first essay, a consideration of the work of the great and newly relevant media critic Neil Postman, was written in 2017. This is not long after Donald Trump, assuming the presidency, brought a new strain of nihilism to old notions of "political theater." Subsequent essays explore life lived under that regime, considering, among other topics, the rise of QAnon, the dark lexicon of the Fox News Channel, the presidential election of November 2020, the Capitol insurrection of January 6, 2021, the Big Lie, misinformation, Tucker Carlson, Britney Spears, Harvey Weinstein, Pete Buttigieg, Marjorie Taylor Greene, *The Masked Singer*, and Attila the Hun. But there is a method, I promise, to the madness. Making sense of this political moment requires a consideration of this cultural moment, too. The essays reflect that. They examine a culture—and, with it, a political environment—that too often confuses reality and delusion.

Propaganda, too, is a theme here: The essays, together, argue for a more expansive appreciation of what political manipulation can involve. Propaganda, in the age of the infinite scroll, encompasses much more than Orwellian inversions and outright lies; it has now taken a postmodern form. The deceptions that angle to mislead us are often refractive and self-reflective and maddeningly difficult to capture. Sometimes, still, they lie out loud; just as often, though, the manipulation works insidiously. Propaganda, the essays suggest, can play out as irony. It can play out as performative apathy. Often, today, propaganda is merely a means of unseeing the obvious, whether facts or feelings or other people's pain.

I was one of the many who, in the aftermath of Donald Trump's election—and in the aftermath of Kellyanne Conway's coinage of "alternative facts"—revisited the writings of Aldous Huxley, Hannah Arendt, and George Orwell. I came to agree with the argument Neil Postman makes at the outset of *Amusing Ourselves to Death*, the book revisited in this collection's first essay: The dystopia that most accurately forecast our fate is not Orwell's *Nineteen Eighty-Four*. It is Huxley's *Brave New World*. In Huxley's vision, Postman noted, "no Big Brother is required to deprive people of their autonomy, maturity, and history." The means of their deprivation is instead, in some sense, themselves. Huxley's great insight is that, through technologies that soothe and distract—delights that keep a public in a ceaseless state of misdirection—"people will come to love their oppression, to adore the technologies that undo their capacities to think."

I shudder, still, when I read that line. I think of the profound exhaustion that can settle in as the world whirs around me, and of my own deep desire, when trying to make sense of it all, to turn the channel. And then I think of another dystopia that helps to explain us to ourselves: *The Hunger Games*. In Suzanne Collins's series, a reality TV show forces 24 young people into a fight to the death—and broadcasts their bloodshed live to the public. The books further the Huxleyian insight: In the universe Collins creates, entertainment gives way not just to self-imposed captivity, but also to state-sanctioned cruelty. Spectacle, for the people of the republic of Panem, works not just as distraction; it also works as permission. It encourages people, frame by frame, to part ways with their own humanity. *The Hunger Games*, propaganda in the guise of escapism, nullifies the distinction between real people and characters so effectively that its viewers are, soon enough, cheering as children murder each other.

Americans have not reached those barbaric levels of callousness. But we are closer than we should be. (Collins got the idea for her story, she has said, when she was flipping through TV channels one night—and was greeted with reality-show footage in one moment, and, in the next, news footage from the Iraq War.) It's so easy, in a world mediated by screens, to see other people as mere spectacles. And it's so tempting, given all that tugs at our attention, to find relief in the distractions. But the final argument of this book is that Americans, for all our many privileges, do not have the luxury of apathy. The problems that face us, and our world, are too grave to be ignored. Attention is a finite resource. It is a precious one, too. Everything—in a community, in a democracy, on a shared planet—will come down to what people choose to give their attention to, and what they choose to ignore. *The hand is quicker than the eye*, the truism of the magic act insists; the task before us is to see what we need to see, even in the daze.

MEGAN GARBER

May 2022

A

ARE WE HAVING TOO MUCH FUN?

April 2017

EARLIER THIS MONTH, THOUSANDS OF protesters gathered at Washington's National Mall to advocate for an assortment of causes: action against global climate change, federal funding for scientific research, a generally empirical approach to the world and its mysteries. The protesters at the March for Science, as scientists are wont to do, followed what has become one of the established formulas for such an event, holding clever signs, wearing cheeky outfits, and attempting, overall, to carnivalize their anger. "Make the Barrier Reef Great Again," read one sign at the March. "This is my sine," read another. "I KNEW TO WEAR THIS," one woman had written on the poncho she wore that soggy Saturday, "BECAUSE SCIENCE PREDICTED THE RAIN." Three protesters, sporting sensible footwear and matching *Tyrannosaurus rex* costumes, waved poster boards bearing messages like "Jurassick of this shit."

There was a time when irony, in the wake of 9/11, was supposed to have died—when Americans, frightened and weary, worried that the world had robbed them of their constitutional right to laughter. They needn't have fretted: Irony—satire—political discourse that operates through the productive hedge of the joke—have not only evaded death in past decades; they have, instead, been enjoying a renaissance. Jokes have informed many prominent, though certainly not all, political protests; they have also, more broadly, come to shape the way people understand the world around them. Many Americans get their news filtered through late-night comedy and their outrages filtered through *Saturday Night Live*. They—we—turn to memes to express both indignation and joy. Jokes, in other words, with their charms and their appealing self-effacement and their plausible deniability (*just kidding!*), are helping people to do the messy work of democracy: to engage, to argue, and, as with Donald Trump, to launch a successful bid for the presidency of the United States.

Scrolling through Instagram to see the pictures from the March for Science, I marveled at the protest's display of teasing American wit. ("Remember polio? No? Thanks, science!") And then I thought of Neil Postman, the professor and the critic and the man who, via his 1985 book *Amusing Ourselves to Death*, argued preemptively against all this change-via-chuckle. Postman wasn't, as his book's title might suggest, a humorless scold in the classic way—*Amusing Ourselves to Death* is, as polemics go, darkly funny—but he was deeply suspicious of jokes themselves, especially when they come with an agenda.

A

Postman died in 2003; were he still with us, though, he would likely be both horrified and unsurprised to see protesters fighting for the fate of the planet with the help of a punnified Labrador—or, for that matter, to see the case for women's inalienable rights being made by people dressed as plush vulvas. He might whisper that, in politics, the line between engagement and apathy is thinner than we want to believe. He might suggest that fun is fun, definitely, but, given its amorality, a pretty awkward ethic. He might warn, with a Cassandric sigh, that there is something delightful and also not very delightful at all about a trio of *Tyrannosauri* who, in the name of saving the world, try their hardest to go viral on Facebook.

Postman today is best remembered as a critic of television: That's the medium he directly blamed, in *Amusing Ourselves to Death*, for what he termed Americans' "vast descent into triviality," and the technology he saw as both the cause and the outcome of a culture that privileged entertainment above all else. But Postman was a critic of more than TV alone. He mistrusted entertainment, not as a situation but as a political tool; he worried that Americans' great capacity for distraction had compromised their ability to think, and to want, for themselves. He resented the tyranny of the *lol*. His great observation, and his great warning, was a newly relevant kind of bummer: There are dangers that can come with having too much fun.

IN 1984, AMERICANS TOOK a look around at the world they had created for themselves and breathed a collective sigh of relief. The year George Orwell had appointed as the locus of his dark and only lightly fictionalized predictions—war, governmental manipulation, surveillance not just of actions, but of thoughts themselves—had brought with it, in reality, only the gentlest of dystopias. Sure, there was corporatism. Sure, there was communism. And yet, for most of the Americans living through that heady decade, 1984 had not, for all practical purposes, become *Nineteen Eighty-Four*. They surveyed themselves, and they congratulated themselves: They had escaped.

Or perhaps they hadn't. Postman opened *Amusing Ourselves to Death* with a nod to the year that had preceded it. He talked about the freedoms enjoyed by the Americans of 1984—cultural, commercial, political. And then he broke the bad news: They'd been measuring themselves according to the wrong dystopia. It wasn't *Nineteen Eighty-Four* that had the most to say about the America of the 1980s, but rather Aldous Huxley's *Brave New World*. "In Huxley's vision," Postman noted, "no Big Brother is required to deprive people of their autonomy, maturity, and history." Instead: "People will come to love their oppression, to adore the technologies that undo their capacities to think."

A

The vehicle of their oppression, in this case? Yep, the television. Which had, Postman argued, thoroughly insinuated itself on all elements of American life—and not just in the boob-tubed, couch-potatoed, the-average-American-watches-five-hours-of-television-a-day kind of way that is so familiar in anti-TV invectives, but in a way that was decidedly more intimate. Postman was a media theorist above all, and *Amusing Ourselves to Death* owes debts, he acknowledges, to Marshall McLuhan and Walter Ong and Daniel Boorstin and Elizabeth Eisenstein and Karl Marx and Lewis Mumford and the general notion that we shape our tools, and thereafter our tools shape us. Mumford's theories of clocks, Ong's theories of speech, McLuhan's theories of everything—there they all are, making an appearance in this argument about the civic threats of laughter. Postman would wind his warnings about the dystopian dangers of television around his own adaptation of McLuhan's aphorism: The medium, he suggested, is not simply the message—it isn't straightforward or self-aware enough for that. The medium, instead, is the metaphor.

And the metaphorical nature of television, Postman argued, has meant that TV and its very particular logic—its assumptions, its aesthetics, its image-oriented and episodic understanding of the world—have found their way into other areas of American cultural life. Postman wrote

Amusing Ourselves to Death early in the presidency of Ronald Reagan (the former actor, he pointed out, had won a second term in a field that included another celebrity, the former astronaut John Glenn); he wrote long after Richard Nixon had made that tentative, awkward appearance on *Laugh-In* ("sock it to meeeee"), and slightly before a relatively obscure governor of Arkansas would prove his ability to lead the most powerful nation in the world by playing the sax on *The Arsenio Hall Show*. He wrote during the time when it was the newly standard practice for national politicians like George McGovern and Jesse Jackson to both prove and amplify their popularity by hosting *Saturday Night Live*.

Postman was writing, that is, just as the amusement impulse was bleeding into nearly every area of American politics, bringing both irony and redundancy to the term "political theater." Gazing upon it all, he was decidedly unamused. He thought all the dramedies were missing the point. He thought they compromised the other things Americans should value in their civics and in their culture: wisdom, principle, meaning. He pointed to the professors in college classes who were considered good teachers only if they could effectively entertain their students. He pointed to the televangelists of the time who brought an infomercial feel to the experience of faith. He pointed to presidential debates people watched not just to hear policy proposals, but to see great performances. "We

x

6   A

may have reached the point," Postman remarked, "where cosmetics has replaced ideology as the field of expertise over which a politician must have competent control."

If the Americans of 1985 had indeed reached that point, and if the Americans of today have surpassed them in the achievement, then it's been a long time, Postman suggested, in the making. To understand the American culture of the moment, Postman thought, you have to go back, beyond the television and the radio and the newspaper, to the telegraph. The buzzing electrical wires laid loosely over the nation in the 19th century—the network that first gave rise to the extremely postmodernist notion of information freed of its context—was in Postman's telling the harbinger and the ancestor of the American media of the 1980s. For Postman, the answer to the first message ever sent through telegraphic wires—the epic and ominous "what hath God wrought"—included CNN and *Star Search* and actors-turned-leaders and, if you project out just a little bit, *Squawk on the Street* and *Fox & Friends* and diplomacy-via-tweet and White House press briefings that claim to share information but instead spread diversion in both senses of the word.

The telegraph, Postman argued, produced news and information that was, for the first time, detached from the rhythms of people's daily lives. Because of the telegraph, someone in Baltimore could read about a scandal in New York, almost as soon as it had done its scandalizing.

Because of the telegraph, headlines—sensational, fragmented, impersonal—became the defining element of American media production. Because of the telegraph, news became instant and easy. "Where people once sought information to manage the real contexts of their lives," Postman wrote, "now they had to invent contexts in which otherwise useless information might be put to some apparent use." The telegraph, for the first time, "made relevance irrelevant."

And it influenced American media, on the whole, to continue in that pattern. The telegraph gave rise to yellow journalism, which found newspapers competing for audience attention not so much via the information they shared, but via the entertainments they offered. It created a media environment that abandoned sustained narrative for more episodic delights—a condition, Postman put it, in which "facts push other facts into and out of consciousness at speeds that neither permit nor require evaluation." Most of all, it gave rise to the biases that still inform our mass media today, creating, he argued, "a world full of strangers and pointless quantity; a world of fragments and discontinuities."

If that sounds familiar, it's because, as Postman would have it, we are still operating in the paradigm created by the telegraph—one that is extremely good at creating in-the-moment merriment and extremely less good at instilling in its consumers a sense of continuity, meaning,

A

and wisdom. It's no wonder, in Postman's reading, that, today, "fake news" has thrived, that "alternative facts" has become a truism, and that American cultural habits are shaped by a fictional genre that goes by the name of "reality."

Postman was a postmodernist who was uniquely suspicious of postmodern thought, and he worried, as Daniel Boorstin had before him, that our images had come unmoored from our fuller realities—and that people, being tied to them, were similarly adrift. He saw a world in which Americans were made pliant and complacent because of their cravings for distraction. He knew that despots often used amusement to soften and systematize their seizings of power. He worried that television—an environment where facts and fictions swirl in the same space, cheerfully disconnected from the world's real and hard truths—would beget a world in which truth itself was destabilized. "In a print culture," he argued, "writers make mistakes when they lie, contradict themselves, fail to support their generalizations, try to enforce illogical connections. In a print culture, readers make mistakes when they don't notice, or even worse, don't care."

In a television culture, he argued, the opposite is true.

Postman romanticized—really, he over-romanticized—print as a paradigm. He celebrated the literacy and erudition of the early American 19th century without paying much attention to the many, many people who were excluded from the era's notion of politics. And he had very little to say in *Amusing Ourselves to Death* about the obvious rejoinder to its arguments: that entertainment, engaging people as it does, can be extremely democratic. Americans have long leveraged the power of the *lol* to effect political change (see the humor that pulses through Thomas Paine's *Common Sense*, or, slightly more recently, the suffragette Alice Duer Miller's 1915 book of satirical poetry, tellingly titled *Are Women People?*). Politically weaponized dinosaurs may be distinct creations of this supremely bizarre political moment; they are also, however, distinctly American.

Still, Postman understood what might come, because he understood what had been. He saw the systems of things. In one way he couldn't have imagined the world of this moment, one in which television, still, defines so much of American life. He couldn't have anticipated how late-night comedians would come to double, in a culture saturated with information, as pseudo-journalists. He couldn't have known that celebrities would be regularly asked to weigh in on the political conversations of the day, or that they would be excoriated for refusing to engage in those discussions. He would have laughed, probably, if he'd heard that the reality TV star who is president promised not to fire his error-prone press secretary because "that guy gets great ratings."

He likely wouldn't, however, have been terribly surprised. Earlier this month, as President Trump launched a military strike against Syria and its leader's crimes against humanity, Brian Williams anchored MSNBC's coverage of the attack, narrating as footage showed U.S. missiles streaking like unsteady stars across the blank night sky. "We see these beautiful pictures," Williams said, seeming to forget, caught as he was in the moment, the people on the other end—people for whom the bombs would be so much more than mere images. Williams quoted Leonard Cohen. He talked, with wonder, about being "guided by the beauty of our weapons." He repeated once more: "They are beautiful pictures."

Neil Postman couldn't have known. But, in another way, he knew.

THE GREAT FRACTURING OF AMERICAN ATTENTION

March 2022

LAST MONTH, AS DELTA FLIGHT 1580 made its way from Utah to Oregon, Michael Demarre approached one of the plane's emergency-exit doors. He removed the door's plastic covering, a federal report of the events alleges, and tugged at the handle that would release its hatch. A nearby flight attendant, realizing what he was doing, stopped him. Fellow passengers spent the rest of the flight watching him to ensure that he remained in his seat. After the plane landed, investigators asked him the obvious question: Why? COVID vaccines, he told an agent. His goal, he said, had been to make enough of a scene that people would begin filming him. He'd wanted their screens to publicize his feelings.

I did it for the attention: As explanations go, it's an American classic. The grim irony of Demarre's gambit— his lawyer has not commented publicly on the incident— is that it paid off. He made headlines. He got the publicity he wanted. I'm giving him even more now, I know. But I mention him because his exploit serves as a useful corollary. Recent years have seen the rise of a new mini-genre of literature: works arguing that one of the many emergencies Americans are living through right now is a widespread crisis of attention. The books vary widely in focus and tone, but share, at their foundations, an essential line of argument: Attention, that atomic unit of democracy, will shape our fate.

Demarre's stunt helps to make these books' case, not necessarily because of a direct threat it posed, but because it is a bleak reminder that in the attention wars, anyone can be insurgent. Americans tend to talk about attention as a matter of control—as something we give, or withhold, at will. We *pay* attention; it is our most obvious and intimate currency. But the old language fails the new reality. The *attention economy* may imply fair trades within a teeming marketplace, people empowered as life's producers as well as its consumers. But in truth, the books argue, that economy makes us profoundly vulnerable. Our time and our care belong to us right up until they don't. One day, a man got on a plane with an apparent desire to hijack attention. His fellow passengers, and then masses of others, were left to contend with all the fallout.

AS I WRITE, THE Russian military is escalating its attacks on Ukraine. Pundits are arguing that Putin's invasion was spurred by American "wokeness." A Texas state agency began investigating parents of trans kids for the purported "crime" of seeking gender-affirming care for their children. A court declared Kim Kardashian to be single again. Zoë Kravitz wore a Catwoman-themed dress to the premiere of *The Batman*. The January 6 committee laid out a potential criminal case against Donald Trump. Colin Jost helped to product-test Scarlett Johansson's new skin-care line. Ketanji Brown Jackson is meeting with senators in advance of her Supreme Court confirmation hearings. A United Nations report warned that climate change's catastrophes are now encroaching so rapidly that without radical intervention, they might overwhelm any effort to mitigate them. The 5,978,096th person has died of COVID-19.

"My experience is what I agree to attend to," the pioneering psychologist William James wrote in the late 19th century. His observations about the mind, both detailed and sweeping, laid the groundwork for the ways Americans talk about attention today: attention as an outgrowth of interest and, crucially, of choice. James, we can safely assume, did not have access to the internet. Today's news moves as a maelstrom, swirling at every moment with information at once trifling and historic, petty and grave, cajoling, demanding, funny, horrifying, uplifting, embarrassing, fleeting, loud—so much of it, at so many scales, that the idea of choice in the midst of it all takes on a certain absurdity. James's definition, at this point, is true but not enough. The literature of attention updates his paradigms for the age of infinite scroll.

In the new book *Stolen Focus: Why You Can't Pay Attention—And How to Think Deeply Again*, Johann Hari interviews James Williams, the aptly named ethicist who is currently a researcher at the Oxford Internet Institute. Williams shares his three-tiered definition of attention. "Spotlight" is the most familiar form—fleeting, targeted, the kind required of everyday tasks (getting dressed, watching a TV show, reading an article on TheAtlantic. com). The second layer is "starlight": the focus one applies to long-term desires and goals. The third layer is "daylight." This form—so named because sunshine allows people to see their surroundings most clearly—is the focus one applies to oneself. It is akin to mindfulness; it's how you know what you want, and why.

The layered framework is familiar; it recalls Freud's triptych model of the psyche, for one, or the distinction, in yogic practice, between *bahya drishti*, an external point of focus, and *antara drishti*, which turns the gaze inward. Starlight, as a pragmatic matter, might look like bullet journals or vision boards. But dreams for the future take on new clarity when they're understood specifically in terms of focus and distraction. So do the web's temptations. Far too often, I find myself mindlessly twitch-clicking on an enticing headline, and then reading, and then regretting. I pay my attention; I instantly wish for a refund. Starlight might help me to navigate just a little bit better. Do I want to spend a portion of my one wild and

A

precious life considering, through the spate of articles about M&M's revamped mascots, the sartorial choices of candy? Maybe so, but at least I can make that decision consciously. Williams's framework emphasizes the deep connections between the now and the later: Distraction in the short term is also distraction in the long. Starlight cannot orient you if you're forever failing to look up for it.

Jenny Odell proposes a similar recalibration in 2019's *How to Do Nothing: Resisting the Attention Economy.* American culture has moved so far from the Jamesian mode of attention—so far from the simple dignity of choice—that our lexicon itself can be misleading. Attention, Odell argues, has become bound up in the same apparatus that remade hobbies into "productive leisure" and that values people's time only insofar as it proves economically viable. The essential problem is not simply the internet; the villain of her story, instead, "is the invasive logic of *commercial* social media and its financial incentive to keep us in a profitable state of anxiety, envy, and distraction."

Odell, similarly, is not opposed to distraction as a very broad category. An artist as well as a writer, she spends much of the book celebrating the value of wandering minds. They are sources, after all, of creativity and curiosity. But there is a stark difference between being open to distraction and being driven to it. (*Doing nothing*, in Odell's analysis, is not the absence of action; it is an act of reclamation. It is an attempt to make free time free again.) The challenge is to wander mindfully.

How to Do Nothing's arguments echo in some of the web's newer vernaculars: *Clickbait, doomscrolling,* and similar terms acknowledge attention as an ongoing struggle. As Tim Wu argues in *The Attention Merchants: The Epic Scramble to Get Inside Our Heads,* attention is ours, yes, but it is *theirs* too—a commodity fought over by corporations that seek ever thicker slices of our psyches. Wu's targets are Facebook, Google, and the many other businesses that reduce humans to sets of "eyeballs" and treat the mind as an extractive resource. The digital industrialists engage in what Wu calls, in full dystopian dudgeon, "attention harvesting"—the reaping of people's time and care, for profit.

Wu published *The Attention Merchants* in 2016. It has earned in the meantime one of the best distinctions a book can hope for: It has grown only more relevant. Wu's ultimate theme, like Odell's, is resistance. Distraction, Wu notes, tends to empower the industrialists and demean everyone else. If people are to avoid life lived at their mercy, he writes, "we must first acknowledge the preciousness of our attention and resolve not to part with it as cheaply or unthinkingly as we so often have. And then we must act, individually and collectively, to make our attention our own again, and so reclaim ownership of the very experience of living."

A

Discussions of attention, sooner or later, can tend toward the polemic: We are spending our time *this way*, when we should be spending it *that way*. *This* is frivolous; *that* is meaningful. One of the valuable elements of these books, though, is that they cede their final definitions to the individual. They echo James's sense of attention even as they complicate it. Wu's appeal is to the dignity of one's own time; Odell repeatedly uses the word *humane*. You have your starlight. I have mine. They're different. They should be.

But attention, in these frameworks, is also political. In the aggregate, attention is a collective good. A distracted democracy is an endangered one. The authors make liberal use of the collective *we*, and the choice functions not as a glib imposition of commonality on a fractured world, but instead as a simple recognition: In a shared polity and a shared planet, our fates are bound together. Starlight, as personal as it is, can be social too. Considered communally, a sense of common destiny might orient our attention to questions both ancient and newly urgent: What kind of country do we want? What kind of people do we want to be?

DURING HIS FIRST STATE of the Union address, Joe Biden called on Congress to aid U.S. service members who were exposed to toxins while they served in Iraq and Afghanistan. Biden's son Beau, a veteran, died of cancer in 2015.

As Biden spoke of illnesses that would put soldiers "in a flag-draped coffin," Lauren Boebert, a representative from Colorado, yelled at him from her seat.

"You put them there. Thirteen of them!" she shouted, seeming to refer to soldiers who had died in Afghanistan last year.

It would not be the only interruption of the evening. Boebert and Marjorie Taylor Greene, of Georgia, repeatedly attempted to wrest attention from the president as his speech went on. The two began by pointedly turning their backs on the president's cabinet as they entered the chamber, allowing Boebert to display the writing on her shawl: "Drill Baby Drill." As Biden talked about immigration, the two began chanting: "Build—the—wall." *The Washington Post* reported that they spent the rest of the speech laughing at some lines and live-tweeting their animosity toward others. ("Here's another way to fight inflation," Boebert tweeted, at one point. "Resign.")

The whole thing had a tautological quality: Lawmakers, elevated to their positions in part by their skill at making scenes, scene-making once more. The dynamics that set in afterward were similarly foreseeable. Nancy Pelosi condemned their behavior (they should "just shut up," she said), and then people wrote about how Nancy Pelosi had condemned it, and the flurry of it all, in the end, served pretty much no purpose save for the political interests of Lauren Boebert and Marjorie Taylor Greene. Fringe views

A

used to stay where they deserved to: on the fringes of things. Now, those who espouse conspiracies get air time—and, consequently, our time—precisely because their errors are so outrageously clickable.

The paradox of attention is that, at any moment, there's a very good chance that it won't seem worth attending to. *Attention*, after all, is so navel-gazy. There are always so many other things—more specific and urgent and obviously worthy things—clamoring for people's focus. But that there's never a good time to think about attention is precisely why we should be thinking about it—right now, urgently. Climate change looms. People's rights are under threat. Books are being banned. The Big Lie, Donald Trump's false claim that he won the 2020 presidential election, keeps lying; disinformation, compounding the chaos, competes for our care just as fervently as all the scattered truths do. The volume of the distractions only grows; like Boebert and Greene's antics, they threaten to drown out everything else. "The Democrats don't matter," Steve Bannon, that noted purveyor of noise, said in 2018. "The real opposition is the media. And the way to deal with them is to flood the zone with shit."

The strategy works. Attention is zero-sum; that makes distraction a potent weapon. The era of attention crisis is also the era that has given rise to "paper terrorism," a flood-the-zone approach carried out with bureaucratic forms and filings. It is the era that finds the Supreme

Court making binding pronouncements about the most intimate areas of Americans' lives not through its standard proceedings, with all their pesky scrutinies, but via the rushed and abbreviated workings of the shadow docket. Activists have boasted about how simple it's been for them to dissolve hard-won voting rights with the flick of a pen, in part because many of the people who would be horrified at the regression are unaware that it is happening at all. "Honestly, nobody even noticed," one of those activists said. "My team looked at each other and we're like, 'It can't be that easy.'"

When people aren't looking, though, it can be. Hannah Arendt, the great scholar of democracy and its discontents, observed that propaganda, pumped out as a fog that never lifts, can make people so weary and cynical that they stop trying to distinguish between fact and fiction in the first place: everything as possible, nothing as true. A coda to her insight is that plain old news can foster the same kind of exhaustion. To combat it, the books that consider awareness as a resource call for a new focus on attention itself. They argue for a particular kind of mindfulness—a collective gaze that detaches from the tumult, looking anew at the body politic, seeking insight and maybe even wisdom.

Our many crises will not be undone quickly or easily. They might not be undone at all. But the first step toward solving them is to acknowledge them as emergencies. The

A

next is to give them the undivided focus that emergencies deserve. The starlight is there, if we remember to look for it. The people move; the constellations don't. If we find a way to focus on what matters, we may be spared the need to admit, to the generations that follow: We didn't mean for it all to happen. But we weren't paying attention.

HOW TO LOOK AWAY

June 2018

"THESE CHILD ACTORS WEEPING AND crying on all the other networks 24/7 right now; do not fall for it, Mr. President."

Ann Coulter, on Sunday, was speaking to that famed audience of one—Donald Trump—in the language whose grammar and idioms both of them understand intuitively: that of the Fox News Channel. But the pundit wasn't informing the world leader so much as she was warning him. And she was concerned, she suggested, not so much for the presidential mind as for the American soul. You may be tempted, she noted to the president and the larger audience, to feel for the children who wail as they are torn away from their families at the American border; resist that temptation. Do not feel for them; they don't deserve it. They're faking it. As Coulter reiterated on Tuesday, in a follow-up interview with TMZ: "They are trying to wreck our country through a political stunt."

The "they" in question is both unspecified and wincingly clear. And the "stunt" Coulter is referring to, of course, is the information that has been coming from America's southern border, in a progression that has become steadily more urgent in recent weeks. Reports of a woman whose infant was ripped from her body as she breastfed. Reports of a man who died by suicide after he was separated from his wife and son. Reports of kids taken from their parents to get "baths," never to be returned. Images of children, separated from their families, their little fists clenched in fear.

The images, moving and still, are searing, in part, precisely because they are images. They capture something in immediate and visceral and urgent terms that words, even at their frankest and most effective, cannot. The Getty photographer John Moore's viral photograph of a 2-year-old girl sobbing as she watched her mother being frisked by an agent of the American government—the pink shirt, the matching shoes, the pudgy cheeks, frozen in an expression of despair and disbelief—is worth many more than a thousand words. The audio of children crying for parents who cannot come to comfort them, recorded inside a U.S. Customs and Border Protection detention facility, is wrenching precisely because it is so raw and so real. And because it is, in its starkness, so profoundly undeniable.

And yet: Ann Coulter has found a way to deny it. Her repeated accusation—"child actors weeping and crying"—is attempting to destabilize not just the facts on the ground, but also another kind of truth: the emotions most humans will feel, automatically, in response to children who cry in agony. Coulter's warning to the world leader responsible for the tragedy, *Do not fall for it, Mr. President*, is a repetition of the logic deployed by some as a matter of moral reflex in response to the otherwise unimaginable, and otherwise inarguable, tragedies of Newtown, and Parkland, and so many others: They're just actors, those people will insist. *It's all fake*, they will assure. This is a moral claim as much as a factual one: *You don't have to act. You don't even have to care. You can look away from this and still manage to look at yourself in the mirror.*

Tragedies that need not be treated as tragedies at all, because the tragedies, in a fundamental way, are false: In one way, certainly, these are extremely fringe ideas. But in another way—an ever more familiar way, as the Overton window flings ever more widely on its rusty hinges—they are not fringe at all. They have been summoned, instead, across platforms that are decidedly mainstream. They have been, as it were, decidedly normalized.

The press conference conducted by Homeland Security Secretary Kirstjen Nielsen on Monday was, overall, dedicated to the proposition that the reporting coming out of the holding facilities along the American border—the audio, the video, the images of tiny bodies held in massive cages—is wrong. ("Don't believe the press," Nielsen said, echoing one of the core intellectual and emotional propositions of Trumpism.) The president himself has embraced the corollary idea to Coulter's claim that the screaming families are actors: that the compassion for them is misplaced. The real tragedy here, he has suggested, is the one perpetrated by Congress/the Democrats/the fake news/an "infestation"—again, an *infestation*—of people who are not American and therefore do not deserve the same level of sympathy that Americans might. Crisis actors of a different sort.

The White House press secretary, Sarah Huckabee Sanders, similarly dismissed the moral questions at the heart of the family separations by suggesting that there is a more sweeping moral code than the fickle workings of your own heart. ("It is very Biblical to enforce the law.") The attorney general, Jeff Sessions, suggested the same. Humans, ever fallible, must practice humility, this logic goes; part of that practice must involve the recognition that even empathy must answer to a higher power. The higher power that insists, despite so much evidence to the contrary, "I alone can fix it."

And so: *You are looking at the wrong thing*, insist the current stewards of the national soul. *You are caring about the wrong thing.* Sleight of hand meets sleight of heart.

In 1977, Susan Sontag wrote about photography—a century-old practice whose cultural transformations, as tends to happen when the slow march of new technologies is involved, had only become clear after decades of human experimentation with the medium. Photographs, Sontag argued, "alter and enlarge our notions of what is worth looking at and what we have a right to observe. They are a grammar and, even more importantly, an ethics of seeing." An extension of those ethics, it has become urgently clear—particularly in this age defined by the new technologies of the internet and social media—is distinctly political: In a democracy, if the people are to have a meaningful say over the world and its workings, those people are, fundamentally, obligated to look. And, much more fundamentally, to see. To avert one's eyes is a privilege that those of us who have the power to act cannot afford to exercise, even when we are complicit in the images. Especially when we are complicit.

But the democratic alchemy that converts seeing things into changing them is precisely what the president and his surrogates have been objecting to, as they have defended their policy. They have been busily appearing on cable-news shows and giving disembodied quotes to news outlets, insisting that the undeniable evidence of suffering, the images and the audio and the tears and the screams, is deniable after all. Actually, as the Fox News host Laura Ingraham insists, the pens holding the humans are "essentially summer camps." And actually, as *Fox & Friends*'s Steve Doocy instructs, the pens are not cages so much as "walls" that have merely been "built . . . out of chain-link fences." And actually, Kirstjen Nielsen wants you to remember, "We provide food, medical, education, all needs that the child requests." And actually, Tom

Cotton claims, it's smarter to think of the bigger picture: child-smuggling, MS-13, drug cartels. It's savvier, the leader is saying, to look away.

This makes for a neat rhetorical trick: the logic of *not in my backyard,* invoked not merely despite the fact that it is happening in our backyard, but because of it. With seed and sod that we ourselves have planted.

Yes, yes, there are tiny hands, reaching out for people who are not there . . . but those are not the point, these arguments insist and assure. To focus on those images— instead of *seeing the system,* a term that Nielsen and even Trump, a man not typically inclined to think in net-worked terms, have invoked—is to miss the larger point. On MSNBC this week, the host Nicolle Wallace noted to *The Washington Post*'s Philip Rucker that "our eyes do not lie with the images we're seeing from the border." He agreed, of course. (What could be more true?) But on the other hand, the powerful people whisper: Maybe eyes can lie, too. The images, the sounds, the video, the stories: Perhaps, instead of telling truths, they are obscuring them. Perhaps they are baiting your emotions. Perhaps they are trying to manipulate you into misdirected empa-thies. Do not fall for it. Do not feel for it.

This is a moment in America in which people are talking, with mounting panic, about the slow encroach-ments of autocracy. One of the truisms of that discussion is the essential role that information plays in a polity that

A

governs itself: A democracy that cannot agree on shared facts is a democracy that cannot do much of anything else. "Fake news," that sweeping claim of meta-propaganda, is chilling precisely because of the chisel it takes to those foundations. And "fake feelings" works similarly: A corollary to a politics of destabilized truth is a politics of destabilized empathy. Dismissals of "child actors" and "summer camps," levied by the powerful, amount to a particular strain of Orwellianism: a kind of emotional doublespeak. They deny what is plain. They aim to addle the head and to baffle the heart. When you hear a little girl screaming for her absent father, you may reply with automated empathy. You may recall, without trying to, those moments when you yourself were small, when you yourself were separated from your own parent, for an instant or the opposite—how impossibly tiny you felt, and how impossibly big the world was at that moment. You may recall, without trying to, all those times that you, as a parent, could not find your child—all the panic, all the fear, all the love frantically seeking its home. You may feel it, just a very little of it, the pain of strangers that is not yours but in another way very much is. You may, in response, do what Rachel Maddow did this week, as she read a breaking-news bulletin about detention centers for very young children that are referred to, in the language of the state, as "tender-age" shelters: Break down. Lose your words. Erupt into involuntary tears.

But such responses are the ones that many representatives of the United States, elected and otherwise, are claiming to be false. You are being duped, they are suggesting—by the hysteria of the biased media, by the cherry-picking of images and truths, by your own easily manipulable humanity. This week on Fox News, Corey Lewandowski, the former manager of Donald Trump's presidential campaign, interrupted a fellow guest's mention of a 10-year-old girl with Down syndrome who had been separated from her mother with a dismissive "womp womp." The heckle was callous and glib and deserving of the *have-you-no-decency* drubbing Lewandowski got, from many, in response. But his dismissal served the broader argument: that the fake news are at it again, trying to turn empathy into gullibility. To express horror at the events taking place at the border, Tucker Carlson said on his Fox show, is to engage in "performance art." It is to capitulate to those who "care far more about foreigners than about their own people." It is to have lost the battle, and with it, the war. This is a matter of *us* and *them,* Carlson is sure. Your own weary heart might counter that the true subject here, as it always will be, is *we*—but your heart, he insists, is wrong.

BOREDOM IS WINNING

February 2020

ON THE NIGHT OF THE Iowa caucuses, responding to a disastrous reporting process that left the event's electoral outcome uncertain, Pete Buttigieg did the same thing several of his fellow Democratic-primary candidates did that evening: He gave a speech to his supporters. The former South Bend, Indiana, mayor talked about optimism, and about change. But he talked about something else as well—something his fellow candidates, acknowledging the night's lack of an official result, had not: He talked about victory. "Iowa, you have shocked the nation," the candidate said, "because by all indications, we are going on to New Hampshire victorious."

The declaration was a curious one, given that the Iowa caucus had been defined precisely by the absence of "all indications," and given, too, that the confusion had robbed the campaigns of any capacity they might have had to deliver a shock. But the speech was revealing in the speed of its spin: "You have shocked the nation." *Shock* is the language of electric injury, and of modern warfare ("shock and awe"), and of insouciant radio DJs ("shock jocks"), and of Donald Trump. It is a term of extremity.

Here it was, though, being casually applied to an electoral outcome that, strictly speaking, did not exist. The results of the Iowa caucus, as of this writing, are still being tabulated; Buttigieg might well emerge with slightly more delegates than his closest rivals. But his preemptive declaration suggests the extent to which shock itself—as an expectation, and as a demand—has diffused into the everyday workings of things. Americans, with our notoriously fickle attention spans, have fallen prey to an expanding assumption: that one of the greatest political sins one can commit is not to be wrong, but to be boring.

The Iowa caucus, as it happened, took place just after the effective conclusion of another historic event: the impeachment trial of President Trump. As Democrats sought to prove that the president had engaged in an astonishing abuse of power—by, allegedly, attempting to coerce Ukraine into investigating his personal political rivals—many Republicans met their arguments with replies of anti-astonishment. The president's allies, over the past weeks, have made great performances of the surprise they have declined to feel in reaction to the trial's revelations. "Gum-chewing, snacking, yawning, and alleged napping could be seen throughout the cramped chamber," the Associated Press reported of the scene during the Senate trial. Rand Paul was observed doing a crossword puzzle. Marsha Blackburn was seen reading a

A

book (Kim Strassel's *Resistance (At All Costs): How Trump Haters Are Breaking America*, she later clarified). Richard Burr reportedly handed out fidget spinners to combat the tedium of it all.

Had a municipal jury shown such overt disinterest in court proceedings, its members would likely have been held in contempt. But a standard jury takes the need for deliberation seriously. And a standard jury does not come armed with talking points that make messaging out of disinterest. "I'm bored out of my mind," Ted Cruz complained. "Sort of unwatchable," Kellyanne Conway, the White House adviser, assessed. Representative Mark Meadows, a close ally of Trump's, offered his dismissal in the form of advice: "I would suggest that the American people, if they could turn their channel and watch something else, that is what they are doing."

Watch something else. The impeachment trial played out on television; therefore, the logic went, it should have played out as a TV show. It should have featured plot twists and cliff-hangers and electrifying revelations. The Republican lawmakers' complaint, essentially, was that the impeachment proceedings played out as precisely what they were: legal processes. And their assumption was that Americans would share in their disappointment. The president's surrogates helped spread the yawning message. *Fox & Friends* host Steve Doocy: "It was unbelievably boring."

Eric Trump: "Horribly boring . . . #Snoozefest." Representative Matt Gaetz: "This defense needs a little less Atticus Finch and a little more Miss Universe." Bill Bennett, a former secretary of education and a current host on the streaming site Fox Nation: "There's no burglary, there's no break-in, there's no tapes, there's no dress, there's no sex, there's no Monica Lewinsky. Interest just isn't there."

These objections are, in their very petulance, savvy. Boredom can work as a political argument because boredom can work as a political concession: It reduces things down until all that matters is an event's capacity to entertain. ("What we will witness today is a televised theatrical performance staged by the Democrats," Republican Representative Devin Nunes told reporters at the outset of the House impeachment hearings, setting the stage for what was to come.) The real questions of the trial were complicated and consequential: matters of executive privilege and its abuse; of violations of presidential power; of state-sanctioned bullying. The real questions cut to the heart of the American Constitution and the American presidency and the rule of law. The real questions were hard. It's so much easier not to engage—to write the whole thing off as bad TV. It's so much easier to change the channel.

And boredom works as the remote. Tucker Carlson, with his bespoke blend of anger and ennui, described the House impeachment hearings as the story of "how some obscure diplomat you've never heard of said something forgettable to an even more obscure Ukrainian government official about a topic that literally has nothing to do with your life or the future of our country." Carlson was referring to Gordon Sondland, President Trump's ambassador to the European Union, who had testified that day that the president had done exactly what the Senate accused him of doing: attempting to engage Ukraine in a quid pro quo. CNN called Sondland's testimony, which was a swerve from his earlier statements, a "bombshell"; *The New York Times* called it "explosive." But Carlson called it, effectively, irrelevant. And his dismissal was both convenient and ironic. Another set of Trump-allied talking points, after all, paint *obscure diplomats you've never heard of* as the opposite of tedious: potential members of the shady "deep state," whose ability to fade into the background is the source of their menace. But a diplomat testifying in the most public setting possible did not fit the earlier talking points, so the points shifted accordingly. Don't be suspicious of this official, Carlson suggested to his audience; instead, simply be bored by him. Because he, and therefore the damning testimony he offered, *literally have nothing to do with your life.*

BOREDOM, THUS WEAPONIZED, SENDS messages about who, and what, is worth one's attention—and about who, and what, is not. Those messages extend far beyond partisan politics. This week, during the New York criminal trial of Harvey Weinstein, Jessica Mann, one of the more than 80 women who have accused the mogul of sexual misconduct, offered searing and graphic testimony about Weinstein's alleged abuse of her. (Weinstein has denied all allegations of nonconsensual sex acts.) Mann told the court about Weinstein's "unpredictable anger." She told the court that Weinstein had raped her, and that, when she saw him again, he had ripped her pants off while screaming, "You owe me one more time!" Mann wept on the stand as she told her story.

Weinstein, meanwhile? He dozed off.

Boredom claims not to care; used in this way, though, boredom cares deeply. Boredom, summoned as a performance, is a talking point in human form—an argument made without words. Attention, in one way, is a relatively straightforward proposition: It is a thing people have, and a thing people give. It is a currency both paid and earned. But attention, as a social good, has a moral valence, too. It shapes what is elevated and what is dismissed—who is seen and who is ignored. Carlson, when he told his viewers that Sondland's impeachment testimony had nothing to do with their lives, was making an ethical argument: He was giving viewers permission not just to ignore the impeachment, but also not to care about it at all. Secretary of State Mike Pompeo sold a similarly aggressive apathy when he attempted to deflect an NPR reporter's questions about the country caught up in the trial: "Do you think Americans care," he snapped, "about Ukraine?"

Harvey Weinstein was making a similar argument when he failed to pay Jessica Mann the meager courtesy of staying awake for her testimony. The man sleeping as the woman cries: This was a tidy encapsulation of a culture that is itself, too often, uninterested in the stories alleged survivors tell. But disinterest is a strategy, too. In a criminal trial as well as an impeachment proceeding, much is said in the decision to look away.

You might expect, as far as impeachment goes, that the president's allies would use everything at their disposal to defend him. You might expect that Republican members of the Senate would prevent witnesses from testifying at a trial and then loudly complain about the dullness of a trial with no witnesses. What you might not expect, though, is that the partisans' professed ennui would also go airborne—that it would be mimicked by those who are not propagandistic in their aims. "Unlike the best reality TV shows—not to mention the Trump presidency itself—fireworks and explosive moments were scarce," Reuters lamented at the hearings' outset. NBC News set a similar tone: "The first two witnesses called Wednesday testified to President Trump's scheme, but lacked the pizzazz necessary to capture public attention."

Pop-cultural outlets, too, professed their dissatisfaction with what happens when the Constitution gets optioned for a series. *Saturday Night Live*'s assessment of the impeachment proceedings began with a declaration that the event had consisted of "two weeks of dry debate and posturing." The show's cold open offered to rectify the dullness, staging for viewers "the trial you wish had happened": a wacky musical comedy.

In August 2016, before Donald Trump had successfully alchemized his reality-TV fame into the American presidency, *Politico Magazine* ran a story examining his appeal. The reporter, Michael Grunwald, spoke with Jason Molina, a "32-year-old Cuban-American Democrat who . . . voted for Obama twice." This time around, Grunwald learned, Molina was planning to vote for Trump. "Trump is fucking crazy, but I'll vote for him," Molina explained. "The whole system is fucked. Why not vote for the craziest guy, to see the craziest shit happen?" He added: "We got ISIS, we got Zika, we got this, we got that. At least Trump is fun to watch."

This is what happens when shock value becomes the only value. "Fun to watch" becomes the main metric that matters. And that standard is spreading. *The New York Times*, transforming itself from "newspaper" to "reality star," recently broadcast its candidate-endorsement process as a jump-shot-filled, *Survivor*-like TV show. CNN, hosting a Democratic primary debate, largely eschewed questions about policy for ones that manufactured clip-friendly squabbles. Robert Mueller delivered his testimony on Russia collusion to Congress, and was criticized for a lackluster "performance." Donald Trump delivered a State of the Union address so deeply false that it reads like fiction, and one of the big headlines to emerge from that event was not that the president had lied to Congress and the nation—that story, of course, is extremely old—but rather that Nancy Pelosi had ripped up a printout of the speech after its delivery. "Like addicts to the world's most unpleasant drug," the *Times* columnist Michelle Goldberg put it in November, "our political class seems to require ever-greater jolts to feel anything at all."

IN THE PROCESS, BOREDOM becomes a chronic condition. And politics, with its intimate and life-or-death consequences, gets judged according to the sheen of its spectacles. The bar for what is interesting gets ever higher, and the goalposts move ever farther, and before long people start complaining about the lack of fireworks shooting out of the posts' innards.

Take, again, the Democratic primary debates that have taken place this fall and winter. Politicians and media analysts alike have routinely dismissed those events as "boring" and "bad" and "like watching death." The complaints are leveled not because the contests have failed to feature discussions of the most urgent concerns of the day, from health care to racial justice to climate change (which carries the threat of, it is worth repeating, actual apocalypse)—but precisely because they have featured such discussions. The problem, allegedly, is that discussion alone, no matter how crucial the topic, is insufficiently entertaining: Even matters of life and death are not, in themselves, interesting in the pyrotechnic way that this moment demands. They cannot do what Pete Buttigieg claimed Iowa had done with its caucuses: "shock the nation." And they are most definitely lacking in "pizzazz." And so, on those terms alone, they are dismissed.

The impeachment of Donald Trump, for its part, has played out as many assumed it would: as a foregone conclusion, as a sham, as a shame. The exercise featured one of the president's lawyers making an argument so extreme and absurd as to be, in fact, shocking: that an executive can abuse his power, if he believes that power to be in the public interest. It featured U.S. senators, alleged members of the world's greatest deliberative body, allowing that argument to win the day. That's the other problem with boredom as impeachment's talking point: It has been profoundly incorrect. The hearings and the trial have been fascinating. They simply have not been fascinating in the way so many pundits wanted them to be. Their fireworks were contained. Their bombs had already dropped. The trial confirmed what was largely known—about a corrupt world leader; about complacent aides;

A

about a government rotting from within. The story of Donald Trump's impeachment is also the story of the world's most powerful nation crumbling into lazy autocracy. That story is many, many things. One thing it is not, however, is boring.

DO YOU SPEAK FOX?

September 2020

ALL HAPPY FAMILIES ARE ALIKE; some unhappy families are unhappy because of Fox News.

You might have come across the articles, or the Reddit threads, or the support groups on Facebook, as people have sought ways to mourn loved ones who are still alive. ("I Lost My Dad to Fox News," Edwin Lyngar announced in *Salon*, arguing that the network has addicted his father to a diet of misinformation, suspicion, and despair. Said another, of her father: "He always seemed to be yelling." Said another, of both parents: "Their toxic anger and resentment is slowly becoming their entire identity.") The discussions consider a loss that Americans don't have good language for, in part because the loss itself is a matter of language: They describe what it's like to find yourself suddenly unable to speak with people you've known your whole life. They acknowledge how easily a national crisis can become a personal one. At this point, some Americans speak English; others speak Fox.

Political theorists, over the years, have looked for metaphors to describe the effects that Fox—particularly its widely watched opinion shows—has had on American politics and culture. They've talked about the network as an "information silo" and "a filter bubble" and an "echo chamber," as an "alternate reality" constructed of "alternative facts," as a virus on the body politic, as an organ of the state. The comparisons are all correct. But they don't quite capture what the elegies for Fox-felled loved ones express so efficiently. Fox, for many of its fans, is an identity shaped by an ever-expanding lexicon: *mob, PC police, Russiagate, deep state, MSM, MS-13, socialist agenda, Dems, libs, Benghazi, hordes, hoax, dirty, violent, invasion, open borders, anarchy, liberty, Donald Trump.* Fox has two pronouns, *you* and *they*, and one tone: indignation. (*You* are under attack; *they* are the attackers.) Its grammar is grievance. Its effect is totalizing. Over time, if you watch enough *Fox & Friends* or *The Five* or Tucker Carlson or Sean Hannity or Laura Ingraham, you will come to understand, as a matter of synaptic impulse, that immigrants are invading and the mob is coming and the news is lying and Trump alone can fix it.

Language, too, is a norm. It is one more shared fact of political life that can seem self-evident until someone like Trump, or something like Fox, reveals the fragility that was there all along. You might have observed, lately, how Americans seem always to be talking past one another— how we're failing one another even at the level of our vernacular. In the America of 2020, *socialism* could suggest "Sweden-style social safety net" or "looming threat to liberty." *Journalist* could suggest "a person whose job is to report the news of the day" or "enemy of the people." *Cancel culture* could mean . . . actually, I have no idea at all what *cancel culture* means at this point. Fox, on its own, did not create that confusion. But it exacerbated it, and exploited it. The network turned its translations of the world into a business model. Every day, the most watched shows of the most watched cable network in the country—with more than 3.5 million viewers on average, a prime-time destination more popular than ESPN—take the familiar idioms of American democracy and wear away at their common meanings. The result is disorientation. The result is mass suspicion. Like a vengeful God bringing chaos to Babel, Fox has helped to create a nation of people who share everything but the ability to talk with one another.

THERE'S AN EPISODE OF *The Office* that ends, as so many episodes of *The Office* do, with Jim playing a prank on Dwight. Dwight, who sells paper with the militant zeal he brings to everything else he does, wins a company-wide prize for his sales record. His reward is to give a speech at a corporate gathering. Dwight is nervous about this opportunity; Jim—here is where he *stares directly at the camera*—gives him some public-speaking advice. Fast-forward to Dwight, in a cavernous hotel ballroom, breathing heavily into the lectern's microphone, pounding his fists, and shouting lines from the script Jim had provided him: the Googled speeches of famous dictators. Jim had turned Dwight into something he wasn't; that was the prank. But the joke was that Jim had also turned Dwight into something he'd been all along. Dwight Schrute has what psychologists might refer to as an "authoritarian personality." Jim had given him, in a roundabout way, the ability to become himself—dictator cosplay, no costume required. The crowd loved it.

I thought of Dwight while watching the first night of this year's Republican National Convention—specifically, while watching Kimberly Guilfoyle deliver her own version of Dwight's speech to living rooms across America. Guilfoyle, a Trump-campaign fundraiser, a sort-of daughter-in-law to the president, and a former Fox star, shouted her speech. She finger-pointed and fearmongered with a verve that might have been comical were it not also, in its Mussolinian menace, terrifying. Of Joe Biden and assorted other "cosmopolitan elites," Guilfoyle said:

> They want to steal your liberty, your freedom. They want to control what you see and think and believe so that they can control how you live. They want to enslave you to the weak, dependent, liberal victim ideology to the point that you will not recognize this country or yourself.

Guilfoyle's script, like Dwight's, was both wildly inappropriate and deeply revealing. It was also, at this point,

A

familiar. Guilfoyle was speaking the language of Fox. Her warnings were lifted from the same text the network's opinion hosts read from each evening: *elites*, *control*, *enslave*. Here was Fox's defining monomyth—the *you* and the *they*, locked in unending combat—brought to party politics' biggest stage.

If you weren't a regular viewer of Fox, Guilfoyle's speech, and the many others that followed it as the convention wore on, might have been nearly unintelligible. If you hadn't been informed that inclusivity is "groupthink"; if you weren't conditioned to understand that the definition of *media* is "the enemy"; if you hadn't been aware that Democrats want to "destroy your families, your lives, and your future"—you might have been jarred by all of the vitriol. You might have found yourself wondering why, in the midst of a global pandemic that had sickened millions of Americans and claimed the lives of more than 170,000, the RNC was warning about the threats of "cosmopolitan elites." You might also have wondered why, during the nation's long-overdue racial-justice reckoning this past summer, the RNC gave airtime to a wealthy St. Louis couple who brandished guns at peaceful protesters—or why, during an economic emergency that has cost millions of Americans their livelihoods, a teenager was trotted out to muse about cancel culture ("being canceled, as in annulled, as in revoked, as in made void").

The speeches, yes, were distractions from the ground truths of our crises. But they also attempted another kind of control: They reveled in the power TV has to shape—and to limit—viewers' empathies. Instead of describing the America that is, the Republican Party described the America that is manufactured, every day, on Fox. It used its platform to refight some of Fox's fondest micro-wars. It told its viewers not to focus on the people who have died, or the many more who might, but instead to focus on themselves: *Your* freedom. *Your* future. *Your* America. Watching it all, I felt the familiar fog that descends when something is lost in translation, when someone talks about something you share—in this case, a country—using details that are unrecognizable. It was the same kind of haze that came when Trump, newly sworn in as president, coined *American carnage* to describe a nation where violent crime had been declining for decades. *Do we live in the same America?* the broken words whisper. *Maybe not*, the same words reply.

When scholars discuss the effects of propaganda, that dissonance is often what they talk about. In his 2015 book *How Propaganda Works*, the philosopher Jason Stanley defines political propaganda as "the employment of a political ideal against itself." He describes in particular how self-negating language can make for self-negating politics. "The most basic problem for democracy raided by propaganda," Stanley writes, "is the possibility that the vocabulary of liberal democracy is used to mask an undemocratic reality." Masha Gessen, the great observer of modern autocracy, writes of a more generalized kind of dissolution: "When something cannot be described," Gessen notes, "it does not become a fact of shared reality." In George Orwell's *Nineteen Eighty-Four*, freedom is captivity, peace is war, truth is a lie. But it is Aldous Huxley who, in a 1936 essay collection, offers the most chilling consequence of facts made foggy: "The propagandist's purpose," he observes, "is to make one set of people forget that certain other sets of people are human."

THE FOX NEWS CHANNEL itself arose as a matter of negation: Rupert Murdoch and Roger Ailes, guided by the Nixonian notion that America's "unelected elite" had amassed too much power, created the network in 1996 as a counterweight to the liberal bias that many conservatives saw in journalism writ large. But Fox's initial project now reads as quaint. War is, at this point, Fox's defining metaphor. Like the other outlets that both inspired Fox and were inspired by it—conservative talk-radio shows, *Breitbart News* and other websites—the network often processes the facts of the world as assorted weapons of war. On Fox, there are enemy combatants (Hillary Clinton, James Comey, "the Media," Nancy Pelosi, Robert

Mueller, Christine Blasey Ford, China, immigrants, Democrats) and there are allies. The sides are always clear. So is the cause.

"For the past five years, I've had a front row seat to the Trumpification of Fox and the Foxification of America," Brian Stelter writes in his new book, *Hoax: Donald Trump, Fox News, and the Dangerous Distortion of Truth*. Stelter, as a media correspondent and analyst, covers Fox for CNN. His book is deeply reported: For it, Stelter spoke with more than 140 staffers at Fox, along with 180 former employees and other people with direct ties to the network. ("Fox did not cooperate with the book," Stelter told *The Washington Post*, but he "was in frequent touch with Fox News spokespeople" for fact-checking and the like.) Many of *Hoax*'s revelations are astonishing, even—especially—if you follow the network. Fox really does function, Stelter suggests, as Trump's presidential daily briefing. (The president reportedly once told the Fox legal analyst Andrew Napolitano: "Everything I know about the Constitution, I learned from you on *Fox & Friends*.") And Fox really does serve as a kind of adviser to its most fervent fan. Trump, Stelter writes, "granted pardons because of Fox. He attacked Google because of Fox. He raged against migrant 'caravans' because of Fox. He accused public servants of treason because of Fox."

The leader and the news network speak, and enforce, the same language. Trump regularly lifts his tweets directly

A

from Fox's banners and banter. Last year, Media Matters for America's Matt Gertz counted the times the president tweeted something in direct response to a Fox News or Fox Business program. Gertz found 657 such instances—in 2019 alone. Fox hosts and producers use that power to manipulate the president. "People think he's calling up *Fox & Friends* and telling us what to say," a former producer on the show tells Stelter. "Hell no. It's the opposite. We tell *him* what to say."

But the manipulation flows in both directions. At Fox, Stelter reports, executives live in fear of angering the opinion hosts, who in turn live in fear of angering viewers—who of course have been made angrier by the hosts themselves. A former producer tells Stelter: "We were deathly afraid of our audience leaving, deathly afraid of pissing them off." Stelter's sources describe "a TV network that has gone off the rails," he writes. "Some even said the place that they worked, that they cashed paychecks from, had become dangerous to democracy." A well-known commentator on the network tells him, "They are lying about things we are seeing with our own eyes." An anchor laments that "we surrendered to Trump. We just surrendered." The capitulation has become so complete, and so widely recognized, that when a Fox news reporter actually questions the president, the questioning itself makes news.

Fox is fond of accusing its alleged enemies of "politicizing" the news; the irony is that politicizing the news is

Fox's most basic move. Take the network's coverage of COVID-19 in the spring. The opinion shows often treated the pandemic not as a public-health emergency, but as a political threat to Trump—as a front in its ongoing war. The Fox host Pete Hegseth: "I feel like the more I learn about this, the less there is to worry about." The host Jeanine Pirro: "If you listen to the mainstream media, it's time to buy the family burial plot." The language mocked, and minimized. Geraldo Rivera announced, baselessly, that if you could hold your breath for 10 seconds, that was a sign that you were COVID-free. On March 6, Fox's longest-tenured medical analyst, Marc Siegel, told Hannity that "at worst, at worst-worst-case scenario, it could be the flu."

Every news network struggled to understand the threat of the coronavirus in those early days. But Fox struggled much more. Stelter quotes several staffers who were ashamed and angry with the network's coverage at a time when it was crucial for Americans to grasp the severity of the virus. "Hazardous to our viewers," one told him. "Dangerous," said another. "Unforgivable," said another. And also hypocritical: Even as Fox was airing segments that downplayed the threat of the virus, Stelter reports, executives at the network's headquarters in Manhattan were ordering deep cleanings of their offices and making preparations for their talent to work remotely. On March 9, Stelter notes, Hannity poked fun at his favorite

A

targets—"Dems," "the Media"—for, he claimed, exaggerating the threat of the virus. "They're scaring the living hell out of people, and I see it again as like, *Oh, let's bludgeon Trump with this new hoax*," Hannity said.

Nine days later? He was insisting that "we've never called the virus a hoax."

War, in the field, rationalizes behavior that would be deemed immoral in times of peace. War, used as language, can amount to a similar kind of exceptionalism. If your side is the right side, you might do whatever it takes to make sure that your side keeps winning. You can justify a lot in the name of liberty. (The title of Hannity's 2002 book, Manichaean and Mad Libbian at once, is *Let Freedom Ring: Winning the War of Liberty Over Liberalism*.) One *Fox & Friends* staffer Stelter spoke with describes being upbraided for a particular piece of copy she'd written for the show: an update sharing the news that White Castle would begin to serve vegan burgers. The copy presented the introduction as a positive development. But that was wrong, the staffer was told: The new burgers were actually part of the "war on meat."

A 2019 SURVEY BY the Public Religion Research Institute tracked the differences between "Fox News Republicans" and other Republicans who said Fox was not their primary news source. Of the Fox loyalists, 55 percent said that there was nothing the president could do to lose their approval. That figure helps to explain how Fox can serve the state even as it operates independently. The "home team" is a powerful thing. Peter Pomerantsev, the author of *Nothing Is True and Everything Is Possible: The Surreal Heart of the New Russia*, points out how cannily Fox employs the metaphor of the family in its packaging of its opinion shows: Bill O'Reilly, Pomerantsev told me, was for a long time the network's cynical uncle. Tucker Carlson is the quirky cousin. Sean Hannity, meanwhile, is "the father coming home, ranting about this horrible world where the white man felt disenfranchised." Familiarity, literally—this is the "strict father" model of political discourse, rendered as infotainment. The upshot, Pomerantsev noted, is a constructed world that is above all "very, very coherent."

Earlier this summer, Tucker Carlson opined that Black Lives Matter is "not about Black lives" but about "left-wing mobs" who are trying to "cancel your rights." He warned viewers to "remember that when they come for you." Some advertisers left; Carlson stayed on the air. He stayed as audio surfaced of him referring to Iraqis, in 2006, as "semiliterate primitive monkeys" and saying, in 2008, that the Congressional Black Caucus existed to "blame the white man for everything." He stayed after he claimed that immigration "makes our country poorer and dirtier and more divided." Fox's PR machine, when Carlson made that comment in late 2018, backed up its star: "It is

A

a shame that left-wing advocacy groups, under the guise of being supposed 'media watchdogs,' weaponize social media against companies in an effort to stifle free speech."

This is the paradox of a certain brand of propaganda. It is not the result of top-down efforts to capture hearts and minds; it is the result, instead, of a powerful entity responding to a powerful public. "No cable operator has ever seriously flirted with dropping Fox to save money," Stelter notes, "because, among other reasons, they believe the right-wing backlash would cripple their business." The president has his base; so does the network. That confers another kind of impunity. Fox can say whatever it wants with little consequence, save for, perhaps, higher ratings. One of the most sobering takeaways of Stelter's reporting is that Fox foments fear and loathing not really because of a Big Brotherly impulse, but because the network has recognized that fear and loathing, as goods, are extremely marketable. In 2020, Stelter notes, Fox "is on a path to $2 billion in profits."

And yet: *You* are under attack, Carlson tells his viewers, with his signature furrow of the brow. *They* are coming for you, he insists. Carlson does what he wants, and says what he wants, because he can. And he suggests that his audience, through the transitive powers of television, can enjoy a similar freedom from accountability. Critics might talk about Fox as an "information silo." They might dismiss the network's skewed stories as alternative realities.

But even the insults, in their way, inoculate. They imply that Fox can do what it does in isolation. It cannot. Its outrages are atmospheric. Its definitions of the world are communal, even if they aren't commonly shared. The events of 2020 have been tragic reminders of that. When cruelty is refigured as "free speech," and when expertise becomes condescension—and when compassion is weakness and facts are "claims" and incuriosity is liberty and climate change is a con and a plague is a hoax—the new lexicon leaps off the screen. It implicates everyone, whether they speak the language or not.

A

DWIGHT SCHRUTE
WAS A WARNING

October 2020

THESE ARE BOOM TIMES FOR the *Lolsob*. Watching the news, I sometimes find myself staring at the screen, eyes wide, brain broken, not sure whether to laugh or cry. The farce and tragedy tangle so tightly that it can be hard to tell where one ends and the other begins. How do you make sense, for example, of a leader who, in the midst of a deadly pandemic, muses about the curative powers of drinking bleach? How do you process life lived under the influence of other people's delusions? The words, after a while, stop working. The categories collapse. Many true things have been written about what living under this regime feels like; one of the truest I've encountered is a 2017 prediction from the writer Hayes Brown: "This is going to be the dumbest dystopia."

Even the escapism acknowledges the whiplash. As people do their *lolsobbing* and doom-scrolling, many are also watching a sitcom that, as one of its executive producers put it, "mixed melancholy and joy in the same space." *The Office* is 15 years old and one of the most consistently popular shows of this moment. Its renaissance has many explanations: The show is streaming on Netflix. Its mock-umentary style—the *directly at the camera* playfulness it brings to its tales of the Dunder Mifflin Paper Company of Scranton, Pennsylvania—gives it currency in the age of the reaction GIF. The series resonates emotionally with those who might be missing their own workplace as offices across the country shutter in response to the COVID-19 pandemic. And it resonates politically through Michael Scott, the boss who is convinced that the solution to any problem is to put on a good show. I'm one of the people who have found new solace in old episodes of *The Office*, but I have a slightly different reason for watching. That reason is Dwight Schrute.

Dwight, Dunder Mifflin's best-performing paper sales-man and its worst-performing person, is a category error in human form. He is a beet farmer in a corporate park, a survivalist selling office products, a 19th-century spirit in a 21st-century timeline. He is arrogant. He is, relatedly, a buffoon. "FALSE," he will say about something that is true. "FACT," he will say about something that is not. He listens to metal but plays the recorder. He defers to the rules right up until he breaks them. Dwight is Darwinism with a desk job. He is anarchy in the guise of law. He is tragedy and he is comedy, and because of that he is intensely cathartic to watch. Many fictions speak to this moment. Dwight K. Schrute, however, inhabits it.

IN AN EXTENDED SCENE in *The Office*'s fifth season, Dwight takes it upon himself to give his colleagues a lesson about fire safety. Summoning the show's roving camera to document the education he is about to impose, Dwight tosses a lit cigarette into a wastebasket he has doused with lighter fluid. "Today," he says, "smoking is gonna *save* lives."

This surprise tutorial goes . . . very badly. As soon as they notice the smoke billowing out from under a hallway door, Dwight's co-workers do exactly what they should during such an emergency—call for help, check for escape routes—only to discover that their phone lines have been cut (by Dwight) and their doors locked (Dwight again). "Okay, we're trapped! Everyone for himself!" Michael screams. Oscar removes a panel in the ceiling and hoists himself up, vowing to get help. Jim and Andy try to use the office's copy machine as a battering ram to bust the locked door open. Their fear is building. The smoke is getting worse. Dwight, to heighten the panic, sets off fireworks in the middle of the bullpen. "The fire is *shooting at us*!" Andy screams. "What in the name of God is *going on*?" Phyllis wails.

What viewers know—and what the workers of Dunder Mifflin soon find out—is that the answer is *Dwight*: Dwight is going on. *The Office*'s writers created the fire-drill scene for an episode that aired after the Super Bowl in 2009. Tasked with writing something that would be legible to football-carryover audiences who weren't already familiar with the show, they resorted to slapstick. The set piece they wrote is brilliant physical comedy. It is also, however, an object lesson: Here is Dwight's defining paternalism turned into a source of injury. Here is Dwight revealing the error of a familiar political refrain: *He's too incompetent to be dangerous.* Dwight's safety training is so deeply unsafe that it ends up giving Stanley a heart attack.

Sitcoms make certain promises to their audience: reliability, relatability, stakes that are soothingly low. But *The Office* played with those assurances. Michael may be the character who gives voice to questions about comedy's boundaries; he's the one who says things like "I hope to someday live in a world where a person could tell a hilarious AIDS joke. It's one of my dreams." But Dwight lives out those tensions. Through him, *The Office* engages in an ongoing act of reckoning: It tries to figure out where, precisely, the comedy ends and the tragedy begins.

In many early episodes of the show, Dwight's destructive tendencies are treated as gentle jokes. He brings weapons into the office; Pam laughs about him being a "gun nut." When he brags about his ability to "physically dominate" other people—or when he remarks offhandedly, "Better a thousand innocent men are locked up than one guilty man roam free"—the message is less that he is a

A

menace than that he is a fool. Dwight comes to work on Halloween dressed variously as the Joker from *The Dark Knight*, a Sith lord, and the local criminal known as the "Scranton Strangler"; the costumes read primarily as pitiable. The sanitized threats are elements of the sitcom's promise: No matter what might happen on the show, viewers can safely file it away as Fun. This is also part of the alchemy through which Dwight Schrute—a misogynist in the age of Elliot Rodger, a conspiracist in the age of QAnon, a vigilante in the age of Kyle Rittenhouse—can read, still, as a joke.

Dwight is finely calibrated. One of his jobs in *The Office* is simply to be odious enough to justify whatever pranks Jim and Pam might play on him. Jim putting Dwight's stapler in Jell-O, or putting the full contents of Dwight's desk into the office vending machine? These are proportional responses, *The Office* suggests. Jim can't cross the line, because Dwight has, perpetually, already crossed it for him. Dwight regularly insults Pam. He steals a big sale from Jim. When a small amount of marijuana is discovered in the office's parking lot, Dwight invokes his status as a volunteer sheriff's deputy to make his colleagues undergo drug testing. "As it turns out," Jim comments, "Dwight *finding* drugs is more dangerous than most people *using* drugs."

To be in Dwight's vicinity is to be at risk, always, of becoming collateral damage. The threat is evident even in the way *The Office* is shot. To realize its mockumentary conceit, the show hired a cinematographer who had just finished filming early episodes of *Survivor*; the resulting camerawork suggests at once constant surveillance and constant over-proximity—all these people bumping into one another. And Dwight, more than any other character on the show, is inescapable. The casting call for the role noted that Dwight's "unpleasant personal habits and annoying personality suggest an unsocialized loner, a sort of Caliban or Gollum." It added: "His lack of social skills render[s] him the butt of office jokes and thus bearable."

But as *The Office* moved into later seasons, the calculus of Dwight's bearability changed its terms: His actions came, more and more regularly, with specific consequences. Dwight, it cannot be stressed enough, *gives Stanley a heart attack*. He traps Meredith in a trash bag with a bat. Even his love life takes on, for a stretch, a sense of menace: The Dwight-Angela-Andy love triangle ends painfully for all parties, in part because Dwight's gaudy version of honor does not preclude his cheating with someone else's fiancée. As the show went on, the comedy around him got darker, too. In Season 4, Dwight speaks fondly about his grandfather, who is 103 years old and "still puttering down in Argentina"; as he talks, it becomes clear to everyone but Dwight that Grandpa Manheim is a Nazi.

To succeed with an American audience, one of *The Office*'s truisms goes, the U.S. version of the show had to

A

be a little bit kinder—a little bit softer—than the acerbic British original. Dwight, modeled after the U.K. show's Gareth, is the character who most directly challenges that idea. He is humor that, at times, hints at horror. Jim spends an episode convincing Dwight that (1) the bat they've discovered in the office is vampiric, and (2) Jim has been bitten by it. This provides an occasion for Dwight to brag about his experience with werewolves. "I shot one once," he says. He pauses. "But by the time I got to it, it had turned back into my neighbor's dog."

Ooooof. In Andy Greene's fantastic oral history, *The Office: The Untold Story of the Greatest Sitcom of the 2000s*, the show's writers describe the debates they had about whether to include jokes like that one. Even comedy carries certain inevitabilities; all the latent violence in Dwight had to erupt, eventually. Late in the series, he realizes his professional dream: He becomes the office's acting manager. He promptly turns the place into a totalitarian regime in miniature (time cards for salaried workers, forced recitations of the Pledge of Allegiance, a framed portrait of himself installed in the reception area). And then, walking around the crowded bullpen with a loaded gun, Dwight accidentally fires the weapon.

The bullet hits the floor. But Dwight, having put all of his colleagues into needless mortal danger, is quickly demoted. The injury he has caused, this time around, is one he has inflicted on himself.

THIS IS WHAT I meant when I was talking about catharsis. Dwight is shameless; *The Office* finds ways to shame him all the same. That simple procedure of cause and effect is remarkable to watch right now, because, in America's lopsided nonfictions, shamelessness often carries no consequences at all. Donald Trump, America's own regional manager, flouts the law in plain sight. He lies with such impunity that *lie* itself, as a diagnosis, becomes banal.

Accountability, in that context, might look like someone doing a bad job and therefore losing their job. It might look like someone compensating for the harm they've caused. But it might also look like fairness of another sort: like Dwight, a danger to his colleagues, being treated as a threat. Or like Dwight, a fool, openly acknowledged as one. A prank Jim and Pam play on him leads to Dwight getting a job interview from a competing paper company. "Look, I'm all about loyalty," he tells the show's camera. "In fact, I feel like part of what I'm getting paid for here is my loyalty. But if there were somewhere else that valued that loyalty more highly—I'm going wherever they value loyalty the most."

The confession has so much specificity. It defines Dwight as exactly what he is: a hypocrite who thinks he's a hero. The actor Rainn Wilson has described the character he played as "someone who does not hate the system, but has a deep and abiding love for it." One of *The Office*'s ongoing jokes, though, is the hollowness of his devotion. "That is the law according to the rules," Dwight says at one point. He does not stop to consider why "the rules" exist, or whom they serve. Dwight embodies the philosopher Kate Manne's observations about white male entitlement: When you assume yourself to be naturally entitled to deference or forgiveness or love, she argues, the assumption self-rationalizes. Power, too, is tautological. In September, a journalist asked Trump about the staggering number of American deaths from COVID-19. "It is what it is," the president replied. Spoken like a true Dwight. The character predicted a world, the writer Sarah Rosenthal observes, that is "defined by anxious men, desperate to feel powerful the way they might have in a bygone era, while insensitive to the humanity of others." And he anticipated a political condition in which hypocrisy would be so widespread—and so absurdly brazen—as to be environmental. Dwight is, in his contours, Mitch McConnell. He is Brian Kemp. He is Donald Trump. He is someone who imposes his will on everyone else and then says, when they object, *That is the law according to the rules.*

Hypocrisy at this extreme is hard to talk about. American political language is simply not equipped to contend with actors who are so Schrutily immune to shame. Pundits continue to describe speeches that Trump manages to recite without some ad-libbed cruelty as evidence of "presidential" behavior. During his "debate" with Joe Biden in late September, Trump lied and yelled and ceaselessly interrupted his opponent. Mike Pence, conversely, in his own debate with Kamala Harris, lied calmly; his performance was categorized as an exercise in civility. Lies are not civil. They are, in fact, the opposite. But this is precisely how hypocrisy can compromise habits of language. Shamelessness changes every equation. That might help explain why the age of Trump has also been an age of category collapse, and also an age of "chaos." Press briefings, these days, are "chaotic." Entire news cycles are "chaotic." I recently found myself describing an omelet I'd made as *chaotic*. The assessment is useful in part because it channels the frenzy of this moment: the speed, the contradiction, the sense of chronic whiplash. But to describe something as chaotic is also to give up on describing it at all. It is to concede to the mess, whether the thing that is breaking is an egg or a democracy.

In that environment, even small acts of clarity can be corrective. When the *lolsob* is a cultural condition—and when *lolnothingmatters* is a constant threat—there's power in a show that reckons with comedy's capabilities. In America today, Nazis are disguising their hatred through perky memes. A U.S. senator, Kelly Loeffler, is making not-so-veiled threats against journalists in a campy ad featuring Attila the Hun. The president is lying and then insisting that he was only kidding. Jokes can be shameless, too. So it's a relief, if only cold comfort, to watch comedy that assumes laughter's limits. By the end of *The Office*'s nine-season run, Dwight Schrute has evolved. His contradictions have resolved into a kind of order. He has come to see his colleagues not as his subjects, but as his equals. The transformation is not inevitable, but it is necessary. An "agent of chaos," his arc has acknowledged, is simply not a sustainable character. *The Office* was wise in many ways, but its greatest insight might be this: It knew when to stop humoring the guy who, in the name of workplace safety, sets the whole office on fire.

BEWARE FALSE ENDINGS

_____

October 2020

EARLIER THIS WEEK, A STRIKING thing happened at the Supreme Court: A justice inserted several errors into the record. The mistakes came as the Court was making last-minute decisions about the precise time span of an election that has been taking place for weeks. The errors were products, as *The New York Times* put it, of "the court's fast pace in handling recent challenges to voting rules." They also emphasized the extent to which the election is being waged through proxy campaigns—through battles that treat voting not just as the voice of the public, but also as a matter of logistics. How will votes be processed? How might they be, right out in the open, suppressed? When will they stop being counted?

And when will this election, technically, end?

News organizations will help answer that last question. That is in part because, as *The New York Times* columnist Ben Smith wrote in August, "the American media plays a bizarrely outsize role in American elections, occupying the place of most countries' national election commissions." As local election boards process ballots and report the results, news outlets—TV news outlets, in particular—will make projections. They will make announcements. And they will be contending with a mess of complications that include, this year, an incumbent president who has made no secret of his desire to sow chaos and confusion as the returns come in. The responsibility held by media organizations, in this context, will be immense: They will need to not only inform their viewers, but also orient them. And explain vote-tabulation processes to people who may not be familiar with them. And debunk—or strategically ignore—any misinformation that is churned out into the mix.

They will also, crucially, need to do something that tends not to come naturally, to human beings in general and to the humans of the press: They will need to accept uncertainty. "When every legitimate vote is tallied and we get to that final day, which will be some day after Election Day, it will in fact show that what happened on election night was . . . a mirage," the CEO of a top Democratic data-and-analytics firm told the news site *Axios* earlier this fall. This is the situation, he argued, that might become clear in retrospect: "It looked like Donald Trump was in the lead and he fundamentally was not when every ballot gets counted."

A scenario like this would pose a challenge to televised news in particular, TV being a medium that thrives on discrete dramas and tidy stories. News programs are organized into segments—episodes that have beginnings and middles and ends. But very little about Election Night

A

will lend itself to such organization. It is very possible, for one thing, that Election Night will not be a single night at all. In that environment, CNN and Fox and MSNBC and the broadcast networks will need to work against instinct. They will need to model patience and calm. They will need to fight the desire to tell stories that have concrete endings.

The Trump administration, for its part, constantly engages in battles for unearned endings. On Wednesday, the White House Office of Science and Technology sent out a press release highlighting the scientific accomplishments it claimed to have achieved over the past four years. One of the items on the list? "ENDING THE COVID-19 PANDEMIC." (On Thursday, the United States reported more new cases of the disease than on any other day since the pandemic began.) The release came soon after the White House, hoping to solidify a conservative majority on the Supreme Court should the election results end up being decided there, rushed the confirmation process of Amy Coney Barrett. (One of Barrett's new colleagues on the bench, Brett Kavanaugh, benefited from a 2018 confirmation process that was similarly beset by manufactured haste. "We're going to plow right through it," Mitch McConnell said of the vote at the time—and that is just what the Senate did.)

News organizations have occasionally abetted the White House in its quests to declare presumptive victory.

Earlier this year, NBC News published an analysis complaining that *the impeachment hearings of the president of the United States* were lacking in "pizzazz." Reuters agreed: "Unlike the best reality TV shows—not to mention the Trump presidency itself—fireworks and explosive moments were scarce," the news service noted with a nearly audible sigh. The assessments were assuming that the most important thing for an impeachment trial to be was not rigorous or careful, but instead exciting. They were arguing, effectively, that a civic event playing out on television should operate as a soap opera. When it did not, they dismissed the whole exercise as evidence of bad TV.

Donald Trump is himself a creature of television. His celebrity was magnified by TV; his reputation as a businessman, buoyed despite his bankruptcies by his role on *The Apprentice*, was laundered by it. And he has brought the underlying logic of television—in particular, its assumption that every day is a new episode that might erase what came before—to his governance of the country. He has treated the White House's coronavirus press conferences, when he holds them, as blank-slate opportunities to recast the day's reality in his preferred terms. Trump treated his own infection with COVID-19 as a nearly sitcomic event: drama and resolution in one easy episode, the ending punctuated by a triumphal declaration that he had been "healed."

A

In May, *Politico* published a story outlining the Trump administration's decision to reopen the American economy despite the ongoing presence of the coronavirus. The administration took that action against the advice of the White House's own health advisers. "There's this mindset that it's like running a show and you've got to keep people tuned in, you've got to keep them interested and at some point you've got to move on and move on quickly," a former Health and Human Services official told *Politico*. "Viewers will get tired of another season of coronavirus."

This is life and death, rendered as a limited series. Its posture assumes that the American attention span is as limited as the president's. It is impatience rendered as public policy. And it has its insights: Americans are, indeed, exhausted. This show has gone on for far too long.

In another way, though, American culture is acclimating to the notion of impossible endings. Cliff-hangers keep hanging. Podcasts tell their tales over weeks and months, punctuating statements not with periods so much as ellipses; they bring the shapelessness of the internet—Facebook feeds and Twitter streams—to their storytelling. It's no surprise that this is also the age of the reboot and the sequel, in which characters come back from the dead so regularly that every person in fiction—or, more cynically, every piece of intellectual property—has the potential to be Lazarus-ed. *Saved by the Bell*, via its revived version on the streaming platform Peacock, has been saved for a new generation. *Supermarket Sweep*, on ABC, is sweeping once more. The website *Insider*, earlier this month, offered a list of "TV reboots, remakes, and spin-offs that are in the works." The list has 25 entries.

That environment of constant churn—that ongoing sense of the ongoing—could prove beneficial should Election Night become Election Week, or even Election Month. Americans have already begun making their peace with uncertainty. We marinate, after all, in anti-endings, in politics and far beyond. "There Won't Be a Clear End to the Pandemic," my colleague Joe Pinsker wrote in September. (Instead, he noted, Americans should expect "a slow fade into a new normal.") The pandemic, that framing acknowledges, isn't a single story—any more than climate change or racial justice or economic inequality are single stories. This has been a time of gradual acclimation to that fact. Endings are seductive. They suggest order, and resolution, and relief. But they don't always reflect the world as it is. Often, they mislead. "The End" can be a conclusion with no real closure—and recognizing that, on its own, will help to prepare us for the days and years to come.

A

AMERICAN CYNICISM HAS
REACHED A BREAKING POINT

February 2021

EARLIER THIS MONTH, AT THE start of his Fox News show, Tucker Carlson shared the results of an investigation that he and his staff had conducted into a well-known agent of American disinformation. "We spent all day trying to locate the famous QAnon," Carlson said, "which, in the end, we learned is *not even a website*. If it's out there, we could not find it." They kept looking, though, checking Marjorie Taylor Greene's Twitter feed and "the intel community," before coming to the obvious conclusion: "Cable news" and "politicians talking on TV," Carlson said, must be responsible for the lies running rampant in America. "Maybe *they're* from QAnon," he added. "You be the judge."

This anti-investigation, like so much of what happens on Carlson's show every day, was funny right up until it was frightening. (Just before informing his viewers of his inability to locate QAnon.com, Carlson had attempted a rebranding of disinformation itself: "Freelance thinking," he called it.) The most basic of good-faith searches would have revealed the reality—and the danger—of a widely believed conspiracy theory positing, in part, that Democrats eat children. But reality is not Carlson's project. Destabilizing it is. Fox's most popular personality, his show's marketing literature will tell you, offers "spirited debates" about the news of the day. In truth, Carlson is simply selling cynicism. Night after night, he informs you that the ways you might have of understanding the world and yourself within it—politics, culture, science, art, the news, other people— are not to be trusted. The only American institution that remains worthy of your confidence, in the bleak cosmology of *Tucker Carlson Tonight*, is Tucker Carlson.

I mention Carlson's act not because it is extraordinary, but because it is banal. *Topple the media* is about as Propaganda 101 as it gets. It's the *Lügenpresse*, it's Newspeak, it's the coup leaders heading straight for the TV station. Cynicism is, among other things, a habit of disordered vision: It looks at friends and sees foes. It looks at truth and sees deceit. Cynicism, at scale, makes democracy's most basic demand—seeing one another as we are—impossible. And America, at the moment, is saturated with it. Cynicism makes daily appearances on Fox (and on Newsmax, and on One America News Network). It was the molten core of Donald Trump's presidency, and the only real message Rush Limbaugh had to give. It lurks in the language of QAnon. It lives in the Big Lie. It seethed in the violence of the Capitol insurrection. It has made suspicion an easy sell. "From falsehood, anything follows," posits a law of classical logic. It is called the principle of explosion.

A

THE ERA OF TRUMP seemed as though it might offer, for a time, a wide-scale reckoning about truth and the facts it comprises. Soon after the United States elected a reality star as its president, George Orwell's *Nineteen Eighty-Four*, that fable of state-sanctioned delusion, rose to the top of Amazon's best-seller list. (One spike in sales came just after Kellyanne Conway, attempting to justify the new administration's lies about its inauguration-crowd size, coined the term *alternative facts*.) The phrase *fake news*, wielded by a president who treated ignorance as an art form, settled into the American vernacular; "The truth is more important now than ever," a *New York Times* ad campaign replied.

But the reckoning, as so often happens, never completed its accountings. What those years primarily achieved was to remind Americans of how profoundly vulnerable they were to those who would try to deceive them. The Russian government, having been caught sowing mistrust in 2016, found a more sweeping means of manipulation in 2020. Fact-checkers noted when Trump told his 1,000th lie as president, and his 10,000th, and finally his 30,573rd. Their labors chafed against one of his presidency's abiding perversions: The more widely accounted his corruptions were, the less accountable to them he seemed. That remained the case even as the casualties of his falsehoods mounted. The lies Trump told about COVID-19 exacerbated a deadly pandemic. The garish fantasies he spread about a "stolen" election proliferated for months. Their result was unthinkable and almost inevitable: A mob, believing the stories it had been sold, attacked the government.

Lies are not semantic. Lies can lead to violence—in some sense, they *are* violence. They are as destabilizing to the social environment as guns can be to the physical: When someone is armed with a willingness to deceive, nobody else has a chance. And cynicism, that alleged defense against duplicity, can have the upside-down effect of making the cynic particularly vulnerable to manipulation. One of the insights of *Merchants of Doubt*, Erik Conway and Naomi Oreskes's scathing investigation into the American tobacco industry's lies about its products, is that the deceptions were successful in part because they turned cynicism into a strategy. Faced with a deluge of studies that made the dangers of smoking clear, tobacco firms funded their own—junk research meant not to refute the science, but to muddle it. The bad-faith findings made Americans less able to see the truth clearly. They manufactured confusion the way Philip Morris churned out Marlboro Lights. They took reality and gave it plausible deniability.

Trump's Big Lie worked similarly. He understood, with the fabulist's blithe intuition, how many people had a vested interest in unseeing the election's obvious outcome. He took for granted that Fox and other outlets

A

would repeat the fantasies so dutifully that soon, in their hermetic worlds, the fictions would seem like facts. Trump's legal team filed 62 lawsuits alleging election fraud and lost 61; the resounding defeats made notably little sound. In early December, *The Washington Post* reported that 220 Republican lawmakers were refusing to say who had won the election. In mid-January, a poll asked likely Republican voters whether they continued to question the election's results; 72 percent said they did.

The Big Lie did not, in the narrow sense, succeed. Joe Biden was inaugurated on the appointed day, and Trump now leads his legions from the craggy shores of Mar-a-Lago. But nor did the lie end. Trump is spreading it, still. Compliant news outlets are giving him a platform to do so. (On OANN, this week, the former president said, "The election was stolen. We were robbed. It was a rigged election." On Newsmax: "We did win the election, as far as I'm concerned. It was disgraceful what happened." On Fox: "Rush thought we won, and so do I.") The merchants of doubt, understanding that "truth in advertising" applies to goods but not to facts, keep right on selling their wares.

Trump's second impeachment trial dwelled within the cynicism, too. Democratic prosecutors presented raw footage of the mob's violence and Trump's incitement of it (video evidence, in a typical trial, being considered a compelling way to prove that alleged events actually happened). Trump's lawyer dismissed the video as the slick work of a "movie company." Here, again, was doubt offered up as a reason to unsee the obvious. The jurors in this particular trial had lived its events themselves. The facts were plain; that didn't matter. Presented with all the evidence, 43 U.S. senators chose instead to look away.

But partisanship! you might say. And I know, I know—you're right, of course. But "partisanship" can be a strain of cynicism too. It can insist that only half the world's facts are worth seeing. And it can claim that there are things more important than truth. "What happens when you're wrong?" Joey, the son of the tobacco lobbyist Nick Naylor, asks in the 2005 film *Thank You for Smoking*. Nick has just given Joey a lesson in the art of unfalsifiable-claim making. Joey has been slow to learn it. "See, Joey, that's the beauty of argument," Nick says. "When you argue correctly, you're never wrong."

EARLIER THIS MONTH, AS a winter storm left millions of Texans without water or power or heat, the state's governor, Greg Abbott, made an appearance on Sean Hannity's Fox News show. Here was the message the leader chose to convey that evening, as his constituents chopped down fences so that they might burn the wood for warmth: "This shows how the Green New Deal would be a deadly deal for the United States of America."

Abbott was manipulating the truth (the claim that the power outages were caused by malfunctioning wind turbines has been thoroughly debunked). But he was also attempting to manipulate people's compassion. The facts were plain: People were freezing. People were dying. Abbott tried to blur the picture. He tried to turn the blunt fact of human suffering into an airy ideological debate. Why focus on the day's emergency when the real crisis is Alexandria Ocasio-Cortez?

The historian Daniel Boorstin, in his 1962 book, *The Image: A Guide to Pseudo-events in America*, described the pseudo-event as a manufactured product: a happening that happens only to be covered by the media. Abbott's appearance was an inversion of that idea. Here, in the storm and its aftermath, was an actual event, real and hard and happening; there was the leader—someone *with direct authority over the course of that event*—attempting to de-manufacture it. Abbott, unable to deny the facts of the crisis, instead sought refuge in cynicism. He stood athwart history, yelling, "Stop looking!"

The Image is often cited, correctly, as an early entry in the literature of post-truth America. But its insights, today, are as relevant to the national heart as they are to the national mind. Boorstin understood how easy it would be for people in power to engage in scaled acts of sleight-of-hand. Misdirection was at play when children were torn from their parents and held in cages at the U.S. border—and when a slew of Fox personalities insisted that the real story was not their suffering, but rather their mendacity. Misdirection is at play when politicians respond to mass murders, carried out by legally obtained weapons of war, with "thoughts and prayers." *Cancel culture*, that oft-invoked apparition, can be a means of misdirection, too: The idea might once have been nuanced but now often amounts to an excuse for strategic unseeing. Summoned cynically, *cancel culture* permits the consequence for harm done to take precedence over the harm itself. It defends the status quo. It is, predictably, a regular topic on Tucker Carlson's show.

Misdirection is everywhere because it works, as a tactic, anywhere: As a general rule, a public that doesn't know how to look at things squarely is a public that is primed to be manipulated. And distorted vision can easily morph into disordered compassion. *Framing Britney Spears*, a new and widely watched documentary, is ostensibly about the star's legal status and the battle over her controversial conservatorship. Its broader subject, though, is the ease with which cynicism can curdle into cruelty. One of the film's most gutting scenes comes early on, as a teenage Spears is interviewed by Diane Sawyer. The journalist treats her like an idea rather than a girl, her questions terse and very personal. (At one point Sawyer asked Spears to comment on the opinion, expressed by a politician's wife, that Spears should be shot for being a bad role model.) The exchange—Spears cried during the interview—sets the tone for the film's thesis: American culture, not terribly long ago, was able to look directly at a young woman in pain and see not a person but a punch line.

"WE ARE ALL THE unreliable narrators of each other's stories," the conceptual magician Derek DelGaudio remarks in *In & Of Itself.* The show, a compilation of his live performances that recently began streaming on Hulu, does for magic what *Nanette*, Hannah Gadsby's transformative comedy set, did for stand-up—and what *Fountain*, Marcel Duchamp's transformative sculpture, did for art. It uses the tools of its craft to question the craft. It talks about magic as a way to talk about trust. DelGaudio, over the course of the show, does card tricks—one of them turns the audience themselves, effectively, into playing cards—and tells deeply personal stories. He offers meditations on what it feels like to be seen, and to be overlooked. He cries. He makes his audience cry too.

In & Of Itself, which premiered off-Broadway in 2016 and ran through 2018, coincided with a time when America was reexamining the interplay between illusion and reality. Now, as Americans reckon with miasmic mistrust, the show provides some clarity about the mechanics of manipulation. The magician understands roughly the same principles that the propagandist does: P. T. Barnum argued that what he was selling, as he charged people for the thrill of being tricked, wasn't really the trick itself; it was the opportunity for them to investigate the terms of the fakery. Audiences didn't want to see the "Fiji mermaid," the creature he billed as a mystical wonder, so much as they wanted to see how Barnum had constructed the lie. Later, Hannah Arendt would find similar insights in her assessments of propaganda and politics: "Instead of deserting the leaders who had lied to them," Arendt writes, people "would protest that they had known all along that the statement was a lie and would admire the leaders for their superior tactical cleverness."

Today, the exhaust of their observations is visible far beyond American politics. Reality TV long ago gave up trying to fool audiences into thinking that its dramas are "real"; instead, the genre presents riddles to viewers, daring them to decide for themselves what is true and what is a lie. (Consider, too, that QAnon works in similar ways.) *The Masked Singer* and its sibling series, *The Masked Dancer*, which just wrapped its first season on Fox, take a similarly forensic approach to entertainment. The singing/dancing competitions feature a series of celebrities in identity-disguising costumes (a monster, an ice cube, a hammerhead shark) who perform routines and are voted off the show, week by week. The point for viewers is to guess their identities before the masks come off.

Entertainment can have a candid kind of eloquence; they're revealing, these ways people choose to spend their time when they're not spending it on something else. The *Masked* franchise is a straightforward competition series in the *American Idol* vein, but it has also spawned a world beyond the television: social-media accounts and message boards dedicated to mining each episode for clues. The franchise has been a hit. That could well be because its solvable mysteries channel some of the frequencies of this cultural and political moment—a drive for knowingness, an assumption of ambient manipulation. It takes for granted that its audiences are experts about the lives of the famous people in their midst. It assumes its viewers' savviness. It is premised on Americans' assumption that they are always, somehow, being a little bit lied to. (Some other recent products of American pop culture: *Big Little Lies*, *Pretty Little Liars*, *Lie to Me*, *House of Lies*, *The Lie*.)

And yet, crucially: The *Masked* franchise rejects cynicism. Its tone is deep, almost saccharine, earnestness. Person and persona, illusion and delusion, suspense and suspicion—these are the distinctions the shows explore each week. A recent episode of *The Masked Dancer* revealed that the moth who had previously shimmied to "Boot Scootin' Boogie" was . . . the former abductee and current child-rights advocate Elizabeth Smart. The reveal was, even for *The Masked Dancer*, pretty shocking. Asked why she had decided to do the show, Smart replied that her grandmother had recently died. "She never let a moment pass her by," Smart said, "and so when this opportunity came along, I thought, *I live a pretty serious life, and I'm going to take this opportunity and just have fun.*"

Trauma, repackaged as a two-step: Is that cynicism, or something else? The celebrities who appear on *The Masked Dancer* will do so, of course, for lots of reasons they won't mention on the show's stage: money, flagging careers, the finicky nature of fame. Onstage, though, the show is coming to the same conclusion *In & Of Itself* is: that there's a crucial distinction between savviness and cynicism. Smart may have joined the show's cast for several reasons, but one of them—maybe even the main one—might just be that she wanted a cathartic reclamation of fun. *The Masked Dancer,* in that sense, is doing the work that many other recent pieces of culture, including *The Great British Baking Show* and *Ted Lasso*, have engaged in with their own varied spectacles. They're trying to teach us to trust one another again.

THE DYNAMICS HERE ARE pretty straightforward; American pop culture, with all this, is reacting to American news culture. It's no coincidence that kind TV, a comforting strain of reality television that is less about topic than tone, rose to prominence as TV news—cable news, in particular—became meaner and more mistrustful. And it's no surprise that Tucker Carlson, who just lived through the same years everyone else did, took as the message of those years that cynicism sells. (One of his recent assessments of "the media": "Imagine a drunken teenage border guard at the crossing between Togo and Burkina Faso shaking you down at midnight as you pass through.")

Carlson talks that way because he can. He implies to his viewers, every night, that they might talk that way too. The world of *Tucker Carlson Tonight* is angry but also very easy. If you reject facts as the instruments of a biased media, you can say pretty much anything, as long as you say it interestingly. If you brand yourself as an entertainer, not a journalist, you can spread falsehoods in the name of fun. Truth has obligations that opinions do not. Fox, the network, is learning that all over again: The election-security firm Smartmatic, its reputation caught in the tangled web Fox wove as it repackaged the Big Lie, is suing Fox for $2.7 billion.

It might be tempting to look at that development and see a measure of accountability—wild claims made answerable, cynicisms squelched by truth. But the suits will not save us. The entertainer answers to no court of law. And he knows that cynicism, a means of seeing nothing, will remain a powerful sell. What will follow the Big Lie? One answer is that Fox News finally found a way to hold Carlson accountable for the role he has played in breaking Americans' trust: Last week, it gave him a promotion.

ARTICLE CREDITS

ABOUT THE AUTHOR

MEGAN GARBER is a staff writer at *The Atlantic*. She writes about television, movies, books, and the intersection of politics and entertainment. The recipient of a Mirror Award for her writing about the media, she previously worked as a technology reporter for Harvard's Nieman Journalism Lab and as a critic for the *Columbia Journalism Review*. She holds a BA in English Literature from Princeton University and an MA in journalism from Columbia University, and lives in Washington, DC.